LAUGH YOUR WAY TO A GREAT DAY

MEDITATIONS AND AFFIRMATIONS FOR THOSE WHO CAN'T MEDITATE

S. ALSTON

Copyright © 2022 by Bloom Publications

All rights reserved.

No part of this book may be reproduced in any form or by any electronic or mechanical means, including information storage and retrieval systems, without written permission from the author, except for the use of brief quotations in a book review.

Disclaimer

The health affirmations and information provided included in this book are for educational purposes only and do not serve as a substitute for professional medical advice.

It is not our intention to suggest that meditation or affirmations are a substitution for consulting a medical professional or healthcare provider about your condition. Please seek advice from a qualified licensed medical professional if you are looking for medical advice, diagnoses, or treatment.

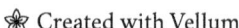 Created with Vellum

For all those who don't let their thoughts stop them from reaching their dreams. You might think you can't do it, but you try again anyway. That's the sign of someone who will get there. You are so close, keep at it! Your future is in your hands.

PREFACE

* * *

Laugh Your Way To A Great Day is a book that explains why meditations and affirmations don't work for some people and offers a new lighthearted way to move you closer to feeling good.

Have you tried to meditate and wonder if it's working? Do you find that you can't sit still, you become distracted or bored, or lose interest? How about affirmations? Have you tried saying affirmations, but they don't seem to work for you? Look no further because this book was created just for you.

With so many meditations and affirmation books to choose from, it can be overwhelming to know which book will be best for you. Sitting in silence can be very difficult for some people, and simply saying positive

PREFACE

phrases over and over again will not work for you if you don't believe what you are saying!

Inside this book, you will find:

- The missing ingredient to understand why meditations and affirmations have not been working for you
- A simple and easy fix to have them start working for you
- A guided laughing meditation that anyone can do
- Health affirmations for anyone looking to heal or reduce pain
- Money affirmations for anyone looking to attract more financial abundance into your life
- Relationship affirmations for anyone looking to improve relationships and/or attract the love of your life to you

The print version of this book has guided meditation and affirmation scripts that you can use to start making the law of attraction work for you. The audiobook will have an enhanced experience because the guided chapters will be set to music, so you can relax and enjoy the full experience. Both are available as choices for you to pick what will work best for you.

PREFACE

This condensed book covers the most powerful aspect of manifesting your dreams and is not intended to be a book that explains the Law of Attraction in full detail. Therefore, it is meant to be concise and provides you with just what you need to know to overcome what has been blocking your path to success.

Congratulations on taking the first step towards making the most of your time when you are meditating and saying affirmations.

Let's get started.

INTRODUCTION

"You deserve to have everything in your life exactly the way you want it." - Jack Canfield

I've spent the last four years learning to meditate to calm my mind. For most of that time, I thought it wasn't working because I never seemed to get to that enlightened place the gurus talk about. Was I doing it wrong? I've felt calm sometimes, which *has* helped me fall asleep. But I was anticipating that at some point, I would see a white light and hear God's voice booming down on me, and that hasn't happened yet. At the same time, I was studying the law of attraction and trying to determine why it doesn't seem to work for everyone. After all, why do positive affirmations work for some people and then not for so many? And while we are at it, why would a loving God seem to grant miracles for some people and not others? I don't think a loving God would do that. It must be something that we are doing

INTRODUCTION

or not doing that is the problem. I don't believe there is a judging God that grants wishes for some lucky people while simultaneously condemning others to live a life of hell. That may sound a little melodramatic, but there *are* so many people who aren't able to create the life of their dreams! Why is that?

What I've come to learn, is that it's not that we aren't *able* to create the life we want, it's that most of us just don't know *how*. And because we don't know how to do it, we actually are using the natural laws of the universe against ourselves and then blaming circumstances, people or places for our failures. It is much easier to blame God or blame others for the misfortune in our lives, but when we do this, we only continue to hurt ourselves. The law of attraction is like the law of gravity. You can't change it, it just is what it is, and you have to work with the laws of gravity if you want to move around in the world. Blaming others for our life circumstances is a bit like a gymnast blaming the beam every time she falls off. She can choose to get back on the beam and practice until she nails her routine, or she can choose to quit gymnastics. But quitting won't ever change her ability to be able to walk or flip on that beam without falling. We all know that it's not the beam's fault that she falls, it's simply that she doesn't know how to do her routine perfectly yet. And with practice, she will. Likewise, when you choose to take responsibility for all your thoughts and actions and start to become aware of how you react in situations and the thoughts you have about it, you are like the gymnast getting back on that beam. And the more you start to become aware and make small changes in your thoughts and behaviors, the more you will begin to notice that things in your life are slowly improving. Keep practicing positive thoughts and actions and you'll start feeling just like that gymnast who has nailed her beam routine.

> **Since there are always two perspectives to view any situation, when we choose to see that the choices we make in every moment create our reality, only then, will we start improving our lives on purpose.**

If we take responsibility for everything that happens in our lives, it means we are no longer victims, we are no longer unlucky, and we are no longer unworthy. It means that there isn't something outside of us that determines whether we get to live a full life. How empowering is that? The fact is, we are all deserving to live the life we've dreamed about and as soon as we fully embrace this truth, that's when the magic of life can begin to work for you as it has for me.

So I wrote this book to help those of you who have been trying and trying to make your life better but seem to keep repeating the same patterns over and over again. If this is you, I commend you on taking the first steps to improve yourself. As you'll find out, this

INTRODUCTION

journey isn't easy, but it is simple. And once you get it (and I promise that you will), the joy you will find in your heart knows no bounds. Things can be going on all around you that would have bothered you before, but now with your slight shift in perspective, you can step back and see the entire picture and realize that the narrow focus you had before was limiting your ability to see the joy that already lives inside of you.

You don't need anyone else, or anything to find it, just you, a desire to find it, and your awareness.

This doesn't mean that I'm a meditating guru now, I'm still finding my way each day. But I can tell you my days have improved significantly since doing this daily practice, so much so that I feel addicted to feeling good! I don't want to feel bad anymore because it just feels too good to experience inner joy. And all of a sudden, synchronicities began to happen. I've met people who love what I'm doing, and I've been able to help them too. It feels like my life is coming together, just as I've planned, which is incredibly thrilling and fulfilling! So I wrote this book to help you find your way a little faster than I have.

Enjoy your journey because you're about to laugh your way to happier days.

THE MISSING INGREDIENT

"A little progress each day adds up to big results" – unknown

So what exactly is this missing ingredient? Most of us have a strong desire to improve our lives; we just don't know how to go about it. We've learned that "it takes hard work to succeed and be happy", and we see successful people being able to afford new shiny things. So many of us grow up thinking that we need to grind and hustle to be able to buy the things we want. Compounding the problem is the belief that material things make us happy. This is where the confusion lies. The truth is that there are many people who work hard, grind, and hustle that have lots of money. But there are also people who don't work hard; they love what they do and wake up every morning loving life because they get paid to do something they already love doing. Then there are people who work so hard and are good people who can't catch a break and are unable to afford the things they want. And then what about celebrities or wealthy people who seem to have it all, a life of wealth or fame and doing what they love every day, yet so many say they feel empty inside? I've always thought how terribly sad it is to hear of someone like that taking their own life because they've been in such a deep depression for years and didn't know how to get out of it. So hard work doesn't always equal lots of money, and lots of money doesn't always equal happiness.

MAYBE WE HAVE IT BACKWARDS. Maybe these beliefs we have are holding us back from seeing the real truth. The happiness we seek doesn't come from material things because material things only provide fleeting pleasure. True joy and happiness live inside us and we find it by tapping into our inner peace, sharing love with others and living out our true purpose. Doing these things is what success is and it's something anyone can achieve, you just have to believe it first.

THE HARDEST PART about the spiritual journey is believing in things we don't see. But having faith in yourself is an essential component to achieving the success you are looking for. This is where meditation and affirmations can help. But for so many people, they want a quick fix, and give up too soon. Let me ask you this question, how old are you? From that age, subtract 10 years since maybe you didn't think the way you do now as a child. What's left is the number of years that you most likely have been practicing the same thoughts over and over again. So whether it's been 10, 20, 30 or even 50 years, it's safe to say it's been a long time. So if it's take many years to get you where you are today, do you think that it may take you more than a few tries to turn your life around? Do you think that you may need to replace your limiting thoughts with new ones and that you'll need to practice them for a while so that they become part of your subconscious mind and your new belief system? So be kind and patient with yourself, and stop taking score too soon.

LET'S say that you woke up one morning and decided that you wanted to learn golf. There were lots of good reasons to pick up the sport, and many of your friends were doing it and saying it was fun, so you decide that you are going to play too. So you head to the driving range to hit some balls. And you are terrible at it. You can't hit very far and the ball goes in all different directions other than where you intend for it to go. So maybe you hire a good trainer to help with your swing. And then it just takes practice to get good.

. . .

Meditation is exactly the same. It might feel like sitting in silence should be easy to master on your first try, but it's actually very difficult for most people simply because we have spent our whole lives thinking constantly and never have tried to "turn off" our analytical mind unless we are sleeping. If you have ever laid in bed worried about something and not been able to sleep, then you know why it can be hard to meditate because it's the same thing.

So what do you do? Well, consider treating your meditation practice like golf. You've already set an intention and decided you want to learn. You've already hired a trainer by buying this book or audiobook. Now all you have to do is practice. And if you feel like you aren't getting better, don't give up! Simply try different techniques or methods and see what works best for you. You'll know if you are doing it right if you feel calm and a little bit lighter after each session. Don't spend a lot of time wondering if you are doing it right and don't take score too soon either because neither of these thoughts serve you. Just remember that Rome wasn't built in a day and Tiger Woods didn't become a golf champion in a week or two. If you want to be good at anything, it takes baby steps to get there. Would you yell at a baby who was learning to walk if he fell down? Of course not! You'd say good job! Try again! So, be kind and patient with yourself as you learn something new. Becoming good at meditation just takes daily practice and the benefits increase exponentially when you start to actually do it regularly.

How do you know if you are doing it right?

Sometimes it's easier to know what you need to stop doing before you can know if you are doing it correctly. If you simply stop doing these things your meditation experience will improve dramatically the more you practice.

- Stop wondering if it's working or not.
- Stop telling yourself you can't do it or that you are doing it wrong.
- Stop complaining that it's not working.
- Stop talking to other people about any of the above.
- Stop judging your ability or how fast you are learning.
- Stop taking score too soon.

INSTEAD, do these things:

- Be open to learning something new even if you think you know how and it "should be" easy.

- Find a comfortable place and get comfortable.
- Decide if you want to sit or lay down, knowing that if you lay down, you might fall asleep (which if helping you sleep is a goal, and you are meditating before bed, then go for it! And celebrate if it helps you sleep! But if your intention is to learn to meditate and consciously restore your body, then stay sitting in a chair or on the floor instead so you don't fall asleep)
- Wear comfortable clothing.
- Relax; this means breathe slow and deep.
- Close your eyes softly.
- Focus on a soft ambient sound or white noise like a clock ticking, the soft hum of a fan in the room, the sound of your breathing or the words of a guided meditation.
- Start to be an observer of your thoughts rather than the one thinking them.
- Simply notice, if your mind drifts to thinking about feeding the dog or what you need to do the rest of the day, and bring your mind back to focusing on your breath.
- Practice doing these things daily and be kind to yourself by allowing space for improvement.

The steps above are nothing new, in fact, every meditation guide will tell you to do those same things. I propose you add one more powerful ingredient that is essential if you want to start manifesting your dreams and feeling good each day.

The Missing Ingredient: Positive Emotion

Our emotions aren't good or bad, they are simply guidance. The first step to understanding why meditations and affirmations don't work for some people is that we are all at different vibrational places in our daily lives. You know how people say "I got good vibes or bad vibes from that person?" That is essentially what I'm talking about. You may not know this, but we live in a vibrational world with frequencies all around us. It's how you watch TV, listen to the radio, use Wifi and so much more. So without diving deep into that subject, just know that everyone has a vibrational set point they practice most of the time. You may go up or down in frequency on any given subject throughout the day, but the one you practice most of the time is your set point. It always begins with a thought, which if you keep repeating that thought, it then becomes a belief. You practice that belief for long enough it becomes an attitude. If you practice that attitude enough it will become your mood, and if you keep practicing that mood all day every day, soon it becomes part of your personality. Your personality influences your behavior and the choices you make on a daily basis which is why your reality is where it is and stays where it is simply because you keep practicing the same thoughts.

THE GREAT NEWS about this is that you can decide to change your set point at any point. It takes just three things to shift your life for the better and start creating the life you want. Once you have all 3 of these things working, you'll begin to notice that your meditations feel more peaceful, and your affirmations start bringing things to you.

THE THREE THINGS ARE:

> *Intention, Determination and the key element most people miss is Positive Feeling.*

IT'S OUR EMOTIONS. Most people have intention and determination down. They may practice over and over and over but nothing ever happens the way they want it to, and the reason is, your feelings are blocking the good coming to you.

ACCORDING TO DR. JOE DISPENZA, your thoughts and intentions are the electrical frequency that you send out into the universe and it's your feelings that are the magnetic force that brings what you want back to you. So most people are sending out signals about what they want and need all day long, but they don't understand the power of our emotions to bring what we want *(and don't want)* back to us.

THOUGHTS ALONE DON'T HAVE much power. It's practiced thought and the feelings you end up having from those practiced thoughts that gain momentum. Just like a car going 1 mile an hour doesn't go anywhere fast, thoughts without feelings attached don't lead you anywhere either. But practicing something over and over, like telling yourself you aren't good at something, can eventually lead you to not liking yourself and thinking you are bad at everything. If this has happened to you, it just means you've practiced a thought over and over and feel worse and worse when you do it, but you never stopped doing it. And now that practiced thought is a bad habit. The good news is that you can start feeling good about yourself again. All it takes is practicing better-feeling thoughts.

SO LET'S assume you agree with what I've just said, but you still find affirmations aren't working for you.

. . .

LET ME ASK YOU THIS. How does it help to repeat affirmations that you don't believe because they clearly aren't true? When you affirm a thought that you believe isn't true, it's like arguing with yourself, and your mind is holding its ground and not budging. For example, if you affirm, I am a millionaire but clearly, you are not, then repeating that statement over and over isn't effective at all because you don't believe it. So the feeling you get from that statement is the opposite. You might think, "This is stupid, I'm not a millionaire, I can't even pay my bills this month!" This is exactly why affirmations don't work for most people, they simply don't believe what they are saying.

HERE'S ANOTHER EXAMPLE. If your practiced thought for the last five years is that you aren't good enough and you suck at learning new things, then you can't simply tell yourself you are amazing 1000 times and fix it if you don't believe what you are saying. This is because practiced beliefs have strong emotions and momentum associated with them. So just like the car analogy, a thought you've practiced for 5 years that makes you feel terrible every time you think it, is like a car speeding down the freeway at 100 miles an hour heading in a direction you don't want to go. You can't turn that around too fast, or you'd crash because the car has so much momentum. You practiced thoughts also have momentum, so first you must slow down before you can turn around. And in order to slow down your practiced thoughts, you need to do two things:

- Stop practicing the thoughts that make you feel bad
- Begin to practice thoughts you believe that make you feel slightly better.

So if you have been thinking, "I don't like myself, I'm terrible." You can't simply listen to an affirmation and say, "I am a wonderful person, I love myself and I light up the world with love, and I inspire everyone I meet," and then magically, you start feeling that way. Your analytical mind will feel the untruth in those statements, and you'll subconsciously argue with yourself inside, which can lead you to think, "see, I'm terrible at meditating too. I can't even sit in silence." Which makes you feel worse!

So instead, try saying,

> *"I'm not always terrible, it's probably more like often or even sometimes."*

Then you could think.

> *"Was there any time in my life that I learned something new?"*

Find that one time in your mind then say:

> *"Of course, there are times I've learned something new. I had to learn how to walk as a baby, I had to learn how to read as a young child, I had to learn to drive and navigate to places I want to go. I've had to learn to cook and care for myself, I've had to learn how to exercise properly and I've learned over time which foods I like best and which ones aren't good for me to eat."*

NOTICE how all of these were true statements, and the positive momentum is starting to pick up? You can probably even list several more recent instances where you have learned something new. Now how do you feel? A little better?

NOW TRY:

> *"I'm open to learning new things. I might not be great on day 1 or 12 or even day 69, but I know I have the ability to try. I also know that I want to make a change in this*

> *area of my life, so just the fact that I'm reading or listening to this book means I'm heading in the right direction!"*

FEEL BETTER STILL?

GREAT JOB! You just slowed down your car enough to turn it around on that subject! Yea! Now you are emotionally much closer to believing yourself when you say:

> *"I'm going to get good at this, in fact I'm getting better everyday. I'm good at learning new things and I'm being patient with myself more often. Things are going better for me, and when new ideas and new opportunities arise for me, I'll know them when I think them or see them."*

IT'S helpful to know that our emotions are not good or bad. They make us feel good or bad, but the emotions themselves are not good or bad; they simply guide us to know if we are on track toward reaching our dreams. Our emotions are simply like the battery gauge on your phone that tells you if you how much power you have left. It's not good or bad it's just information, so you know if you need to plug in or not. When you are running low of energy or feeling annoyed, irritated, anxious, frustrated, angry, or fearful, these are signs that you are thinking thoughts draining your energy and life force. That's why you feel so bad when you practice these thoughts.

You may have valid reasons for practicing the thoughts that make you feel bad, but now that you know your practiced thoughts create your reality, is it worth giving up your dreams to continue feeling annoyed and angry, or fearful about things outside of your control?

This is a huge question to consider. Is it worth being angry at that person or circumstance if you know that anger is the very emotion that tells you you are going the wrong way and you are draining your energy? It's like the GPS system in your car; you wouldn't get mad when it tells you to turn around because you've gone off course from where you want to go. Your emotions are the inner GPS that lets you know if you are heading in the right direction toward what you want. And the better you feel, the faster you'll get there. The worse you feel, the faster you'll get to where you don't want to be.

. . .

So let go of trying to control others and trying to control circumstances. And stop blaming others for triggering feelings you don't want to experience. This is what is really difficult at first, but the more you practice stepping away in the middle of an argument and being to notice that you've reacted to something in a way that has always resulted in a bad outcome, you have turned your car around and are now heading in the right direction. And you'll know it because you feel a little bit better! Celebrate those baby steps because the more you do it, the easier it gets. Set your intentions for the outcomes you want and do everything you can to feel better emotionally. That's how you will have more life force, more energy, and more love to give others, and when you feel that good, you will be magnetically drawing everything back to you.

For a lot of people, this is easier said than done. How do you feel good when bad stuff is happening around you? How do you not get annoyed when you obviously are?

The answer is you don't. You simply become aware of what's happening and then take a break, remove yourself from the place or situation and then do everything you can to be calm and breathe. This will stop the negative momentum from building up and making things worse.

. . .

Put your attention on something else that does make you feel good and you'll notice you start to feel better immediately, and that thing or person won't have the emotional hold on you anymore. You've gained control back.

The more you do things like meditate or practice gratitude and affirming thoughts, the more your emotional set point begins to rise. And there will come a time when those things that used to bother you no longer will. You won't take things so personally, and you'll be less reactive to situations and to people around you because you have shifted your perspective and have clarity like never before.

THE EASY WAY TO ADD POSITIVE FEELINGS INTO YOUR MEDITATION AND AFFIRMATIONS

"The two most important days in your life are the day you are born and the day you find out why." – Mark Twain

In the last chapter we discussed a little bit about how different emotions have different frequencies and how it's nearly impossible to go from a very negative frequency to a very positive one. The built-up momentum makes it too hard to spin your car around. The reason this is so is because the vibrational frequencies of a very low emotion and a very high emotion are just too far apart. And law of attraction won't let you jump frequencies. You have to gradually bring yourself to better-feeling thoughts. Think of a pendulum swinging from one side to the other, as it builds momentum it swings farther and farther from the middle. The pendulum must always swing from one side to the other it can't simply skip the middle and get to the other side.

So imagine a clock face and there is a pendulum instead of the clock hands and the pendulum can swing from 11 o"clock to 1 o'clock and 6 o'clock being the neutral space which can represent feelings of satisfaction. The negative feelings like, boredom, annoyance, irritation, frustration, pessimism, worry, blame, anger, guilt, rage, revenge, to powerlessness and fear are all on the left side of the clock. Boredom would be just to the left of satisfaction and fear would be the furthest away from satisfaction. On the positive side, there are feelings like hope, optimism, worthiness, confidence, happiness, enthusiasm, inspiration, joy, gratitude and love. Picture hope being just to the right of 6 o'clock, and love being all the way at the 1 o'clock position. In this figure below, it illustrates someone who's practiced set point is around satisfaction. It's somewhat easy to go from irritation or annoyance at times on things, and on other things they might feel empowered and they can get to feeling happy without too much effort. *(If you have the audiobook version of this book, these illustrations are included in your downloadable pdf on audible.)*

Now imagine someone who practices worried and fearful thoughts all the time, their practiced set point has shifted their dial so the pendulum rests around worry. It probably doesn't take that person much to be angry or irritated, they may often feel depressed because they can't ever seem to find a happy thought. If you look at the figure below, you can see why. Optimism, happiness all the way to love and appreciation or gratitude is just too far away. So you can't tell that person to just be positive or be grateful and expect them to magically feel better. Their emotional set point is very far from all the positive feelings. And they can't get to joy and happiness from where they are *without* going through all the other emotions first. They might be able to swing to annoyance or irritation instead of anger if they try, but it will take a lot more practiced positive momentum to shift their dial to reach gratitude and love consistently.

A Worried Set Point

THE MAGIC *really begins to happen* when you start to shift your emotional set point toward love. The more you practice better feeling thoughts, you turn your dial and everything around you can begin to change. What you are reaching for is "better feeling" thoughts not necessarily good thoughts. They may be "good" but if you have been stuck in guilt for a long time, anger or blame actually feels better than guilt! And that's good! Think some of those thoughts that are slightly better so you can release the guilt, then remember to keep moving on. You don't want to stay in anger or blame, so move to pessimism or frustration instead. You can keep doing this until you might say:

> *I'm bored with thinking these thoughts anyway.*
>
> *I don't have control over the entire situation, just how I feel about it, and I'm going to choose to let it go for now.*
>
> *I'm even hopeful that maybe things could get better if I just give it some time.*
>
> *It's only been a few minutes and I feel better already. I'm glad I have the ability to make myself feel better in any moment.*

So in this example, that person went from anger all the way to empowerment with just a few thoughts. One that felt slightly better than the next. Baby steps.

. . .

Keep up the baby steps and you'll be running in no time.

Notice how in the following figure, your new emotional set point is now happiness. You've practiced finding better-feeling thoughts so often that the pendulum naturally rests in a good feeling place. If it's resting on happiness, t's so much easier to get to optimism and inner peace and it doesn't take much momentum at all to reach gratitude and love. Now negative feelings feel very far away from you because you don't live close to those feelings anymore; you have shifted your dial and tuned into happiness instead. Now the positive feelings have become your natural state of being. This is truly where you are meant to be most of the time.

Your New Set-Point

Is there a fast way to shift our set point?

There is one way to speed up the positive momentum and get the pendulum swinging to the other side. This is what I want to introduce to you in this book, and it's something that you won't find in most other meditation books. This ingredient is so powerful it can feel like magic.

. . .

So what is this magic ingredient? It's **laughter**. Even if you are feeling pretty down, if you saw something that you thought was funny, you might chuckle or smile, and that action releases some of the negative energy you are holding inside of you. That's why you feel a little better. But if right when you are done laughing, you practice your negative thoughts again, those negative thoughts and feelings will take you back to despair. Now that you know laughing helps you release negative energy, you can practice laughing instead. The more you intentionally laugh, your negative feelings won't have to have so much momentum anymore because you've turned the dial and shifted your vibrational set point to a better feeling place.

We really should laugh more often.

We've all heard the saying, laughter is the best medicine, and it's true. Laughter, like nothing else, can draw strangers together and bond friends and family. This is because it triggers emotional and physical changes in the body. When we laugh, our feel-good chemicals called endorphins are secreted throughout our bodies, which decreases stress hormones, relieves tension and stress, and can actually leave your muscles relaxed for up to 45 minutes after a good hearty laugh! Laughter improves blood flow, so it's great for the heart, and it improves your resistance to disease because of its ability to reduce stress hormones. Laughing can even reduce your pain levels! If you start practicing daily laughing and make that chronic, you may find that your chronic pain or chronic condition starts to ease up because of all the reasons mentioned. This is how people can self-soothe and self-heal. While laughing is in no way a replacement for seeing a licensed physician, regular practice can support your healing process and aid in your ability to reach your health goals and live a happier, more joyful life.

THE NEXT 4 chapters are guided meditations, and the audiobook version enhances the experience; however, self-guided meditations will work just as well. Simply do them with your eyes open, reading the words as you listen to soft music. You can find free meditation tracts on YouTube by searching HTZ. Once you repeat this meditation several times, you may not need to read them any longer, it will be easier to guide yourself. You could also join a partner and take turns reading the meditation script while listening to soft music. Be sure to read slowly and leave ample time to answer questions in your head.

GUIDED LAUGHING MEDITATION

"Start where you are. Use what you have. Do what you can." – Arthur Ashe

*T*his meditation will guide you through practicing the physical aspects of laughter along with intention setting and questions to help guide you so that feeling positive emotions will be easy for you. Practice actually chuckling and laughing may feel forced and silly at first, but once your body warms up, it will feel like a welcome release. And you'll most likely have a massive smile on your face! Feel good knowing you are releasing resistance in your body and moving your emotional set point upward. The more you practice laughing; the more authentic your laughing will be!

. . .

Now,

- Find a comfortable place and get comfortable
- Decide if you want to sit or lay down,
- Wear comfortable clothing
- Close your eyes softly
- During the meditation, listen to the words, and follow along. If you start thinking about other things, just notice, don't judge and bring your mind back to focusing on the words and the music. When you do this you'll be in the present moment.

Let's begin.

Set your intention for this meditation

Say to yourself - I want to laugh and feel good.
It's fun to laugh.
My body likes to laugh.
I'm releasing resistance and negativity when I laugh.

Now Take a deep breath and breath in fill up your belly.

Imagine your belly is a balloon and you are filling it with air.
Now let it go and breathe out.
One more time.
Breathe in 1, 2, 3, 4
Breath out 1,2,3,4

AGAIN
Breathe in 1, 2, 3, 4
Breath out 1,2,3,4

NOW IMAGINE that you are breathing all the way from your low belly all the way up to your brain

Imagine the breath going up your spine as we count to 7.
1,2,3,4,5,6,7
Now let it go
7,6,5,4,3,2,1

AGAIN
Breathe all the way from your low belly all the way up to your brain

Imagine the breath going up your spine as we count to 7.
1,2,3,4,5,6,7
Now let it go
7,6,5,4,3,2,1

. . .

Now breathe normally as you imagine each part of your body relaxing.
>   Your feet are really relaxed.
>   Your ankles are relaxed.
>   Your legs are now relaxed.
>   Your knees are relaxed.
>   Let go of any and all tension in your legs.
>   Your thighs are relaxed.
>   Your pelvis is relaxed.
>   Your abdomen rises and falls; it is relaxed.
>   Your chest is relaxed.
>   Your shoulders are relaxed.
>   Your arms and hands are relaxed.
>   Your fingers are relaxed.
>   Your throat is relaxed.
>   Your head is relaxed.
>   Your mouth is relaxed.
>   Your eyes are relaxed.
>   Your forehead is relaxed.

Now practice smiling and holding a smile for 7 seconds while you breathe all the way up your body again.
>   1,2,3,4,5,6,7
>   Relax

. . .

AGAIN

Hold a smile for 7 seconds while you breathe all the way up your body again.

1,2,3,4,5,6,7

Relax

NOW PRACTICE SAYING the words hee hee hee hee hee hee as you smile and breathe out.

Take a deep breath in

hee hee hee hee hee hee

BREATHE in

hee hee hee hee hee hee

BREATHE in

hee hee hee hee hee hee

Now practice *laughing* the words hee hee hee hee hee hee as you smile and breathe out.

Take a deep breath in

hee hee hee hee hee hee

S. ALSTON

BREATHE in

        hee hee hee hee hee hee

BREATHE in

        hee hee hee hee hee hee

NOW PRACTICE SAYING ho ho ho ho ho ho
   Take a deep breath in

        ho ho ho ho ho ho

BREATHE in

        ho ho ho ho ho ho

BREATHE in

        ho ho ho ho ho ho

Now practice laughing like Santa Claus! ho ho ho ho ho ho

Take a deep breath in

ho ho ho ho ho ho

BREATHE in

ho ho ho ho ho ho

BREATHE in

ho ho ho ho ho ho

NOW I WANT you to try and make yourself chuckle as you breathe out

Breathe in.

Chuckle for 10 - 20 seconds

BREATHE in

Chuckle for 10 - 20 seconds

Breathe in

Chuckle for 10 - 20 seconds

Now imagine that someone just told you something funny or you saw something funny.
    And we'll do it again.
    Breathe in

Chuckle for 10 - 20 seconds

Breathe in

Chuckle for 10 - 20 seconds

Breathe in

Chuckle for 10 - 20 seconds

Now I want you to practice fully belly laughing for 10-30 seconds.
Breathe in

Ha ha ha ha ha ha haa

Breathe in

Ha ha ha ha ha ha haa

Breathe in

Ha ha ha ha ha ha haa

Now imagine that you at a park and there are children giggling and laughing all around you.
And we'll do it again
Breathe in

Ha ha ha ha ha ha haa

Breathe in

Ha ha ha ha ha ha haa

BREATHE in

Ha ha ha ha ha ha haa

NOW RELAX and smile for as long as you can.

REPEAT TO YOURSELF :

>*Today is a new day.*
>*I'm doing things that serve me today so I can feel better.*
>*I'm going to notice when I feel bad and remember that I can change that feeling.*
>*I can think of something else.*
>*I can do something else.*
>*I'm already making positive changes in my life by laughing today.*
>*I feel good.*
>*Good things are coming to me.*
>*I'm going to notice them when they come.*
>*Today is going to be a great day.*

HEALTH AFFIRMATIONS

"Too many of us are not living our dreams because we are living our fears." – Les Brown

If you spent a day writing down all the thoughts you had during that day and then read them back to yourself, I wonder what you would learn about yourself? Do you think that you would find that your self-talk is a lot more negative than you think it is? If your life isn't going well for you, then I encourage you to do this simple test and see. Because you will immediately become aware of thoughts you think that are not serving you. You don't have to be afraid of your thoughts, simply become aware of what you are saying in your head most of the time. If you notice that you are seeing things from a negative perspective or you find that you blame others or spend a lot of time justifying why you can't do this or do that, then set an intention that you want to shift this. Saying the following affirmations will help.

THESE AFFIRMATIONS ARE SPECIFICALLY CHOSEN because you will most likely agree with what is being said. If you notice that something doesn't sit well with you, that means there is some resistance. You can simply change the statement to a question instead. When you agree subconsciously, feeling positive emotions will be easy for you. Instead of saying statements, I'm going to ask you, " how would you feel if……….. this were true?" I want you to imagine the feelings of it happening for you now, and if it were true, then, how would you feel?

FEELINGS ARE the magnetic force that draws everything you want to you, so feel with your whole body. Really get into it and try to imagine what it would feel like if what I'm saying is true for you. Feel good knowing you are releasing resistance in your body and moving your emotional set point upward when you do this. The more you practice these affirmations, the more you will start feeling better each day, the more you allow all good things to come to you.

GUIDED **Meditation Script**

This experience is enhanced in the audiobook,

however you can still read this meditation yourself while you listen to soft music and relax. I suggest that you go to YouTube and search HTZ and find a tract that you like best.

Now:

- Find a comfortable place and get comfortable.
- Decide if you want to sit or lay down.
- Wear comfortable clothing.
- Close your eyes softly.
- During the meditation, listen to the words, and follow along. If you start thinking about other things, just notice, don't judge and bring your mind back to focusing on the words and the music. When you do this, you'll be in the present moment.

Let's begin:

Set your intention for this meditation:

- I intend to practice positive thinking to improve my life experience and to heal my body.
- I know that the more I do it the faster the improvement will come.

- If I miss days though, I won't judge or be hard on myself because that doesn't serve me.
- I'm ready for positive changes in my life.
- I am ready to feel my best.

SAY THESE AFFIRMATIONS SLOWLY, breathe in between each line, and try to feel the feelings that come when you say the words:

> *I am here.*
> *I am getting comfortable.*
> *How would I feel if I was really comfortable?*
>
> *I think I'd be relaxed.*
> *What does it feel like to relax my body?*
>
> *If my feet were really relaxed, what does that feel like?*
> *If my ankles were relaxed, what does that feel like?*
> *If my legs were relaxed, what does that feel like?*
> *If my knees were relaxed, what does that feel like?*
> *If my thighs were relaxed, what does that feel like?*

If my pelvis were relaxed, what does that feel like?
If my abdomen were relaxed, what does that feel like?
If my chest were relaxed, what does that feel like?
If my shoulders were relaxed, what does that feel like?
If my arms were relaxed, what does that feel like?
If my hands and fingers were relaxed, what does that feel like?
If my throat were relaxed, what does that feel like?
If my head were relaxed, what does that feel like?
If my mouth were relaxed, what does that feel like?
If my eyes were relaxed, what does that feel like?
If my forehead were relaxed, what does that feel like?

I'm here.
I'm glad I'm here .
I'm learning to relax my body.

When my body is relaxed it is restoring life energy I need.

*I'm taking care of my body right now.
It feels good to know I'm caring for my body.*

What would it feel like to have a completely healthy body?

*Fit body?
Strong body?
Flexible body?*

What would it feel like to fit in my favorite clothes?

I can imagine me healthy strong and fit.

The fact that I can imagine myself being healthy strong and fit means that it's a possibility for me in the universe.

Spending time practicing calm, positive thoughts is good for my body.

*I am doing things that are good for my body.
I am going to notice when things feel good.*

Now I want you to think of 5 areas of your body that are healthy and strong. And feel gratitude for those 5 areas.

Do you have eyes that can see? If yes, feel gratitude for this. If you have partial eyesight be grateful for your partial ability to see things around you. If you cannot see, practice feeling gratitude for your other senses.

Do you have a heart that is beating? Thank you for my heart that is beating and keeping me alive.

THINK of 3 more areas of your body that work really well and express gratitude for them working well without needing any help or intervention from you.

Say now:

> *My body knows how to heal itself.*
> *When I cut my finger, I don't need to tell my*
> * body to heal it, it just does.*
> *My body wants to heal.*
> *My body wants to feel good.*
> *From now on, I'm going to do things that*
> * support my body's ability to heal.*
> *That includes thinking positive thoughts.*
> *I'm going to stop worrying about my health.*
> * I'm going to know that my body is*
> * working on it.*
> *I'm going to stop taking score too soon and*
> * trust that in time, I am getting better.*
> *I'm going to notice the little improvements my*
> * body is making even if it's only a 1%*
> * improvement.*
> *Because 1% improvements add up over time.*
> *I'm taking time everyday to laugh and to*
> * quiet my mind so my body can help itself.*

Now think of the one area that isn't working well right now and say,

> *I look forward to this area of my body healing.*
>
> *I know that it is a possibility because miracles happen all the time for other people.*
>
> *That means it can happen for me too!*
>
> *What I'm doing right now is bringing that possibility to me.*
>
> *How amazing will I feel when I am completely healthy?*
>
> *What would I do if I were completely healthy?*
>
> *It feels good to think about me living my best life.*
>
> *What does my best life look like?*
>
> *I'd do more fun things.*
>
> *I'd connect with more people.*

I'd say I love you more often.

I wouldn't waste energy on things I can't control.

I'd make the most of my time here on this planet.

Imagine all the people just like me, that I could help when I start feeling better.

They just need encouragement, just like I did, so they keep moving forward toward feeling better.

I'd feel radiant and empowered and joyful, knowing I did this!

I like feeling radiant and empowered and joyful!

When I feel joyful I laugh!

I love laughing.

MONEY AFFIRMATIONS

"Build your own dreams, or someone else will hire you to build theirs." – Farrah Gray

Wherever you are in your financial journey, it's probably true that you would like more of the financial abundance to flow to you! But how *many* ways do you think money can flow to you? Don't limit yourself to thinking that money can only come from your job. Free yourself from that thought and instead adopt the mindset that abundance is everywhere and that there are an infinite number of ways that it can flow into my experience. If this is a statement that is difficult for you to believe right now, don't worry! The affirmations included throughout this book are specifically chosen because you will most likely agree with what is being said. If you notice that something doesn't sit well with you, that means there is some resistance. Simply change the statement into a question. When you agree subconsciously, feeling positive emotions will be easy for you. Instead of saying statements, I'm going to ask you questions instead: " how would you feel if……….. this were true?" I want you to imagine the feelings of it happening for you now. How would you feel if it were true for you? Capture that feeling and hold it as long as you can.

FEELINGS ARE the magnetic force that draws everything you want to you, so feel with your whole body. Really get into it and try to imagine what it would feel like if what I'm saying is true for you. Feel good knowing you are releasing resistance in your body and moving your emotional set point upward when you do this. The more you practice these affirmations, the more you will start feeling better each day, the more you allow all good things to come to you.

GUIDED **Meditation Script**

This experience is enhanced in the audiobook, however, you can still read this meditation yourself while you listen to soft music and relax. I suggest that you go to YouTube and search HTZ and find a tract that you like best.

. . .

Now

- Find a comfortable place and get comfortable
- Decide if you want to sit or lay down,
- Wear comfortable clothing
- Close your eyes softly
- During the meditation, listen to the words, and follow along. If you start thinking about other things, just notice, don't judge. Bring your mind back to focusing on the words and the music. When you do this, you'll be in the present moment.

Let's begin:

Set your intention for this meditation:

- I intend to practice positive thinking to improve my life experience and to allow abundance into my life.
- I know that the more I do it, the faster the improvement will come.
- If I miss days though, I won't judge or be hard on myself because that doesn't serve me.
- I'm ready for positive changes in my life.

- I am ready to hear ideas that allow me to receive all the abundance that is flowing to me.
- Whenever a door closes for me, it is my intention to trust and have faith that something better for me is right around the corner.

SAY THESE AFFIRMATIONS SLOWLY, breathe in between each line, and try to feel the feelings that come when you say the words:

Wherever I am in my life, it's where I am.

I can always choose to make things worse or I can make things better.

It's up to me.

When I blame others for how I feel, I'm a victim and that doesn't feel good.

I have the ability to take charge of my life.

I like knowing that I can be in charge.

I might not know exactly how things will turn

out every step of the way, but I know that when I go on a road trip, I don't need to know every turn ahead of time, either.

What would it feel like if I knew that life was working out for me?

Is there a time in my life when life was working out for me?

Are there things in my life that I really wanted, that I now have?

Life has worked out for me sometimes.

And now that I know what I've been doing that's been blocking it, I can turn things around.

It feels really good to know that.

I find it amazing that the earth and planets are all aligned just perfectly.

I don't need to tell the sun to rise or the moon to come out.

I don't need to tell the plants to grow or the rivers to flow.

There is so much abundance in the world that happens without me having to do anything.

That abundance is all around me.
It's time I started aligning with that abundance.

I'm ready to align with the abundance that is flowing to me.

How would it feel if I knew life was abundant?

How would it feel if I knew money was flowing to me?

What would I do if I had more money?

What would I buy?

What if I had more than enough to buy everything I wanted? How would that feel?

What would I do with all that money then?

Who would I help?

How would it feel to be able to help them?

Are there simple ways I can help those people now that don't cost money?

I wonder if there are ways I can do that?

How would it feel to feel safe?

How would it feel to know everything always works out for me?

I'm tapping into the feelings that bring the abundance of life to me and I can do this anytime I want.

The more I tap into the faster it flows.

I recognize the abundance because it first comes to me as really good ideas that excite me.

When I get a good idea, I write it down.

I won't try to figure out the HOW, right away and bring in my doubt.

I'm going to just let those good thoughts and ideas percolate and grow.

Sometimes I'll have an impulse to do something or to go somewhere, and I might meet that perfect person that can help me expand my idea.

I'm ready for life's synchronicities to happen for me.

I'm eager for that to happen.

And until it does, I'm happy knowing I don't need anything right at this moment to feel good because I can think thoughts that make me feel better.

I feel good.
Life is good.
Life is abundant.

Thank you for this abundant world that I live in.

RELATIONSHIP AFFIRMATIONS

"If you don't like what you are reaping, you had better change what you have been sowing." - Jim Rohn.

It's easy to react to something nice, but it's much harder to maintain you calm mood and feel good when there are situations or circumstances happening around you that you don't necessarily like. But in every single moment, you are sowing seeds that you will reap later. So if you find that you react to life and spend a lot of your energy being angry or upset, then you are sowing seeds that will bring to you more circumstances where you can be angry and upset even more. The universe is based on attraction. So every single thing you put your attention on, the universe thinks that you want more of it, because you are paying attention to it.

. . .

WHEN WE FALL IN LOVE, or when we meet someone new, we tend to notice the person's good qualities. We give them the benefit of the doubt when conflicts arise, and we share our feelings of appreciation with them. So it's no surprise that you become more attracted to this person when you do this. And it's not because the person makes you feel like this; you feel so good because you are using this person as your reason to focus on and give thoughts of love and kindness!

SO IN ANY SITUATION, as long as the relationship is not physically or mentally abusive, you can use gratitude as a way to start paying attention to the positive aspects of that person and your love will grow for that person. As you begin to express more appreciation for that person, they will feel your love and the entire dynamic of the relationship can begin to improve. However, I mention this caveat, because as you move your emotional set point to be more positive, the other people in your life may not be a vibrational match to you any longer; which means you will naturally move away from each other. So work on yourself, and feel more gratitude and appreciation for those people in your life. Find something good in everyone, and the people that don't resonate with the "new you" will drift away, and new people can come into your life.

. . .

IF YOU DON'T HAVE a significant other yet, don't focus on that. Focus on the loving relationships you DO have and give gratitude for them first. Rest in the knowing that your true love is out there and when you are ready for them to come into your life, they will.

JUST AS IN the last 2 chapters, the affirmations in this chapter are specifically chosen because you will most likely agree with what is being said. If you notice that something doesn't sit well with you, that means there is some resistance. Simply change the statement into a question instead. When you agree subconsciously, feeling positive emotions will be easy for you. Instead of saying statements, I'm going to ask you, " how would you feel if……….. this were true?" I want you to imagine the feelings of it happening for you now. How would you feel if it were true for you? Capture that feeling and hold it as long as you can.

FEELINGS ARE the magnetic force that draws everything you want to you, so feel with your whole body. Really get into it and try to imagine what it would feel like if what I'm saying is true for you. Feel good knowing you are releasing resistance in your body and moving your emotional set point upward when you do this. The more you practice these affirmations, the more you will start feeling better each day, the more you allow all good things to come to you.

. . .

GUIDED MEDITATION SCRIPT.

This experience is enhanced in the audiobook, however, you can still read this meditation yourself while you listen to soft music and relax. I suggest that you go to YouTube and search HTZ and find a tract that you like best.

Now

- Find a comfortable place and get comfortable
- Decide if you want to sit or lay down,
- Wear comfortable clothing
- Close your eyes softly
- During the meditation, listen to the words, and follow along. If you start thinking about other things, just notice, don't judge. Bring your mind back to focusing on the words and the music. When you do this, you'll be in the present moment.

LET'S BEGIN:

SET your intention for this meditation:

- I intend to give gratitude for the loving relationships I already have in my life right now.
- I intend to look for things I appreciate in the people around me more often.
- I will voice my appreciation to others more often without needing a compliment in return.
- I know that the more I do it, the faster my relationships will improve.
- If I miss days, I won't judge or be hard on myself because that doesn't serve me.
- I'm ready for positive changes in my life.
- I am ready to hear ideas that allow me to experience the joy of friendship and love with others.
- I am ready to meet new people and experience new things.
- I am open to possibilities that I don't know about yet.
- The more I practice, the more I will know that good things are always flowing to me.

SAY THESE AFFIRMATIONS SLOWLY, breathe in between each line, and try to feel the feelings that come when you say the words:

When I was born, I was pure love.

That love is still inside me.

It feels good to know it's still there.

I used to think that I needed love from other people to feel good about myself, but now I'd like to know that while it's great to get love from other people, that's not where my source of love comes from.

The source of my love comes from me.

If I love myself first, then I have more love for others.

I know that I can't get miserable enough to find love.

Just like I can't get poor enough to help people get rich.

I can't get confused enough to help people find clarity.

It starts with me.

Starting today, I'm going to love myself more.

I'm going to be nicer to me.

I'm going to tell myself I'm a good person.

I'm going to be my own cheerleader and feel good about my baby steps to move forward.

Because that takes courage.

And I am strong.

I didn't know how strong I was until now.

It takes courage to try and improve myself.

Most people won't take the time or effort to do it.
But I am doing it.

It feels bad to blame others for how I feel.

It feels better to know that I'm in charge of my thoughts and feelings.

I like the feeling of empowerment.

The more I do this the more confidence I have in myself.

Confidence doesn't come from somebody outside myself.

Confidence comes from being open to doing new things and then practicing them until I'm good at them.

I can do that.

I do that all the time.

There are lots of times when I've felt really good about myself.

How does self-confidence feel?

How would it feel to feel that way all the time?

How would it feel if I truly loved me?

It feels really good.

I deserve to feel good.

I am a good person.

Loving myself means I take care of me.

When I love myself, I give others permission to do the same.

When I love myself, I'm less judgmental, I'm less reactive, and I'm less opinionated.

Everyone deserves to have their own opinions.

I don't need to fix other people or change their opinions.

Their opinions are not who they are, they are just beliefs they hold.

Everyone has their own inner guidance.

I don't need to try and change other people to be who I want them to be.

I can simply accept who they are and know they are trying to make their own way and do the best that they can.

When I love myself, I'm more compassionate and forgiving.

When I love myself, I allow better relationships to flourish around me.

When I love myself, I do things that support me.

I eat healthy foods more often than not.

I move my body.

I drink water.

I find things that make me smile each day.

I search for things to laugh about each day.

I love having friends.

I love having a family.

I appreciate my friends.

I appreciate my family.

When I love myself it's easier to appreciate everyone else.

When I love myself, I shine bright.

When I love myself I attract people to me.

When I love myself, I give freely.

I don't need to wait for others to give to me first because I just love to give.

I don't need anything in return because I'm connected to the love inside me.

When I look for the good in people rather than

their flaws, I am seeing who they really are.

When I look for the good in me, I am doing the same for me.

When I love myself, my relationships get better and better.

When I love myself, that's when my true love comes to me.

I love to give love.

I love this feeling of empowerment and confidence within me.

I love my family.

I love my friends.

I love making new friends.

I love meeting new people.

I'm excited for the new relationships that are coming to me.

Good things are in store for me.

EPILOGUE

* * *

"When everything seems to be going against you, remember that the airplane takes off against the wind, not with it." – Henry Ford

I hope you enjoyed this book and that it helps you know that you *can* meditate and you *can* make affirmations work for you. You deserve all good things in life and by practicing things that empower you and make you feel good, you are on your way to drawing them to you.

PLEASE TAKE a moment to leave a review if you enjoyed this book. As an independent author, I read each one of them and would so appreciate knowing your story and how these meditations and affirmations help you.

IF YOU ARE a parent or grandparent of young children, you may enjoy my empowering books for kids. Go to www.bloompublications.com Books That Help Kids Bloom And Grow

IF YOU WANT to learn more and continue on your spiritual journey, please follow these inspiring leaders that have together helped hundreds of thousands of people in the world through their life-changing works. Each of these books has helped me grow and find immense peace and joy, and it's my wish that you are able to do the same.

BLESSINGS TO YOU.
    Untethered Soul By Michael A. Singer
    The Power of NOW By, Eckhart Tolle
    The Secret By, Rhonda Byrne
    Becoming Supernatural By, Dr. Joe Dispenza
    The Vortex By, Abraham Hicks
    The Success Principles™ By, Jack Canfield

LAUGH YOUR WAY TO A Great Day

Meditations & Affirmations For Those Who Can't Meditate
By, S. Alston
©2022 S. Alston

RESOURCES

Canfield, J., & Switzer, J. (2015). *The Success Principles(TM) - 10th Anniversary Edition: How to Get from Where You Are to Where You Want to Be* (10th Anniversary ed.). Mariner Books.

Dispenza, J. (2022). *Joe Dispenza Collection 3 Books Set (Becoming Supernatural, You Are The Placebo, Breaking The Habit Of Being Yourself)*. Hay House.

Hicks, A. (2022). *Abraham Hicks Vortex, The Teachings of Law of Attraction and Attract Wealth, Health, and Happiness*.

Singer, M. A. (2012). *The Untethered Soul: The Journey beyond Yourself* (Large type / Large print). ReadHowYouWant.

The Secret by Rhonda Byrne (2006-11-28) (1st (first)). (2022). SIMON & SCHUSTER UK.

Tolle, E. (2004). *The Power of Now: A Guide to Spiritual Enlightenment*. New World Library.

www.ingramcontent.com/pod-product-compliance
Lightning Source LLC
Chambersburg PA
CBHW020332010526
44119CB00002B/29